THE MARTYRDOM OF ST GEORGE EL MOZAHIM

A TRANSLATION OF THE ARABIC MANUSCRIPT

SAINT SHENOUDA PRESS

THE MARTYRDOM OF ST GEORGE EL MOZAHIM

A TRANSLATION OF THE ARABIC MANUSCRIPT

TRANSLATED AND INTRODUCED

BY: DR YOUNHANNA NASSIM

ST SHENOUDA PRESS

SYDNEY, AUSTRALIA

2023

The Martyrdom of St George El Mozahim

Translated and Introduced
By: Dr Younhanna Nassim

ST SHENOUDA PRESS
8419 Putty Rd,
Putty, NSW, 2330
Sydney, Australia

www.stshenoudapress.com

ISBN: 978-0-6457703-7-7

Cover Design:
Dionysia Tanios
@dionysiandesigns

Contents

Translator's Introduction

The Martyrdom of St. George El Mozahim

TRANSLATOR'S INTRODUCTION

The Theology Of Martyrdom

One of the first authors who developed a theory about the theology of Martyrdom is Ignatius of Antioch (end of first century). In his Epistles, he conceives martyrdom as the perfect imitation of Christ, hence true disciple of Christ is one who is ready to sacrifice her or his life for Him. From the Passion of Perpetua and Felcitas, we find another aspect of martyrdom as a second baptism, an idea that was later described as baptism by fire.[1]

The Martyrs Of The Coptic Church[2]

The martyrs of the great persecution may categorize as follows:

1- The martyrs of Egypt a The clergy:

---

1 Youhanna Nessim Youssef, "Martyrs and Martyrdoms in Christian Egypt," A New History of African Christian Thought, from Cape to Cairo, D. Tonghou Ngon, (ed.), New York- London: Routledge 2017, p. 67-77.

2 Youhanna Nessim Youssef, "Christianity in Egypt, the Coptic Church," The Routledge Companion to Christianity in Africa, E. Bongmba (ed.), New York and London: Routledge Taylor and Francis 2016, p.45-60.

This category is very important. Historically, we have the martyrdom of Phileas bishop of Thmui. The Coptic calendar includes also several bishops such as:

Sarapamon, Bishop of Nikiou (28 Hatur),

Pisoura, Bishop of Masil,

Macrobius of Nikiou,

Psate, Bishop of Psoi,

Gallinicus, Ammonius.

b The nobles. c Soldiers:

Apa Dios (25 Tubah),

Abakradjon, (25 Abib),

Saint Menas. (15Hatur)

The martyrs of Antioch,

(The Basilides Family).

This group of martyrs is considered as members of a legendary family of Basilides, king or noble. There are several genealogies included in their martyrdoms but without any consistency.

2- This cycle includes the martyrdoms of Claudius, Basilides, Apater and Iraaie, Macarius, Eusebius, sometimes Theodore, Victor, Besamon, Apoli, and Justus.

3 The cycle of Julius of Akfahs.

This cycle is attributed to a person called Julius of Akfahs. In fact, the study of this corpus shows that these martyrdoms were written from the sixth to seventh century to the eleventh century. The study of the events, administrative titles, geography, and persons demonstrates that we can subdivide this corpus into homogenous groups.

The first group is the martyrs related to the Middle Egypt, such as Epima, Shenoufe, Heraclides, Didymus, Pansnew, Chamoul. It shows that the compiler knew the geography of this district very well; they have a common beginning and end, but there is an evolution towards the presentation of Julius of Akfahs.

The second group is Ari and Anoub, written in Lower Egypt. Julius is presented in a few lines and the author did not give any useful data for the geography of administrative titles.

The third group is Paese and Thecla. It has a different style. It is the story of a brother and a sister, and it seems that the text we have is a compilation of at least two narrations.

The fourth group. Is the martyrdom Macarius of Antioch and Nahrawa . This group is characterized by exaggeration; hence the judge is the emperor himself, and the events are in Antioch (the capital).

The martyrdom of John and Simon is from the eleventh-Thirteenth century and ascribed to Julius of Akfahs.

There are also several texts in Arabic attributed to Julius of Akfahs but it is hard to determine their authorship. We can mention Apa Mirhch, Apa Ischyrion and Kastor.

4 The foreign martyrs a The Post Diocletian martyrs, Alladius (3 Baunah).

b The non-Roman martyrs, St George, James Intercicus, Helias.

c The martyrs of the heresies (against Arianism, Chalcedonianism).

d The new martyrs (or martyrs during the post-Arab conquest). These include John of Phanidjoit, Salib, (3 Kihak), George al-Mozahim (19 Baunah). The text of their martyrdom is more or less realistic – we do not find outstanding miracles, atrocious tortures or heroic answers. The general schema of these martyrdoms is either the saint was accused to renounce to the Islamic faith (some of them adopted the Islamic religion for a while or were from Islamic origins – George al-Mozahim – or through proselytism). An outbreak of the mob or fanatical caprice of some rulers, searching for a scapegoat, caused the martyrdom of these saints. Geographical and historical data are, generally speaking, accurate. e The Confessors such as Agapetus (24 Amshir).

The New Martyrs

The "new martyrs" are those who suffered under Muslim rule. According to O'Leary

"For the most part the Coptic Church did not fare ill under Arab domination, save in suffering financial exactions. Most of the civil service remained in Christian hands and the Coptic patriarch was generally reckoned the wealthiest person .in Egypt, whilst several of the Fatimid khalifs used to retire to Coptic monasteries for a country holiday and were entertained right royally. The prominence of the Copts in the civil service was the cause of much unpopularity, partly the dislike naturally felt towards those responsible for collecting the taxes, partly an impression that they were favoured by government. From time to time, therefore, there were popular outbreaks against the Copts, and occasionally an unpopular governor tried to seek the good-will of the people by leading attacks upon Christian officials and so diverting criticism from his own conduct: there was no regular or consistent persecution of Christians, although, as in all Muslim lands, the penalty of death was incurred by any Muslim who abandoned his religion and embraced Christianity. Occasionally there were sufferers whose martyrdom was due to a local outbreak or the fanatical caprice of some particular ruler, and those who suffered death in such circumstances are described by Coptic writers as 'new martyrs'[3].

Among the New Martyrs, we can mention the name of the monk Mīnā born around the First half of 10th century, the place of his birth is unknown however the Lower Egypt may be probable.

The Martyrdom Of George Muzahim[4]

The author of the text:
little is known about the Coptic Christian author of the martyrdom of Jirjis (named Muzāhim before his baptism as a Christian) other than the little that can be gathered from the text. According to the copy of the Arabic text in Cairo, Coptic Museum – Hist. 469, the author of the martyrdom was one Mīnā, who assures his hearers that he was an eyewitness and a faithful reporter of events (f. 329v). Earlier in the work, a monk named Mīnā had visited the martyr in prison in the Delta town of Damīra, and anointed him for burial (f. 327v). While there is some disagreement concerning the date of the martyrdom, a marginal note in the Arabic text (f. 328v) agrees with the published Ethiopic version

We will give in full what professor Mark N. Swason wrote in the important tool of the Christians- Muslim relations:

"Muzāhim ibn Jāmi was the son of a Muslim Bedouin father and a Coptic Christian mother; his story is set in towns in the Nile Delta. Fascinated since his childhood with his mother's religion, as a very young man he decided to convert to Christianity. He

---

3 De Lacy O'Leary, The saints of Egypt, London: Society for promoting Christian knowledge, New York, MacMillan 1937, p.21

4 Mark N. Swanson, "Martyrdom of Jirjis (Muzāhim)," Christian Muslim Relations A bibliographical history, vol. 2 (900-1050), D. Thomas and A. Mallett, (eds), History of Christian-Muslim Relations volume 14, Leiden-Boston: Brill 2010, p 461-62

married a pious Christian girl named Sayūlā, and – despite some difficulties (including, before his marriage, an attempt at auto-baptism) – he was eventually baptized and received the name Jirjis (George).

Almost immediately upon embracing Christianity, Jirjis was denounced to the local authorities in Damīra and was arrested, interrogated, and beaten; his wife was also maltreated. Constrained to flee from town to town, the pious couple was eventually able to enjoy three years of peace and ascetic devotion (in Tandatā = T ant ā according to The martyrdom; in Saft al-Turāb according to the Synaxarion). At the end of this period, however, Jirjis was again seized and hauled before the authorities in Damīra. He patiently bore maltreatment, beatings, and threats, and rejected blandishments intended to induce him away from his Christian faith. The martyrdom of Jirjis is full of heavenly visitations in prison, remarkable recovery from injuries, and speeches in which Jirjis confesses his Christian faith. Eventually he was beheaded, on 19 Baūna (13 June in the Julian calendar), probably in 978. Signs and wonders were attributed to his relics, and churches were built in his honour.

It may be worth emphasizing that the saint's name was Muzāhim, who after his baptism became Jirjis; I have thus spoken of 'the martyrdom of Jirjis (Muzāhim)'. The form 'Jirjis al-Muzāhim' that is often seen in the literature is best avoided.

While the work is extant in Arabic, the possibility of the existence of a Coptic martyrdom is not to be ruled out.

Significance:

If Arabic was indeed the original language of The martyrdom of Jirjis (as seems probable), and if the 10th-century date of composition is to be taken at face value, then we are dealing with a very early Arabic-language composition of the Coptic

Orthodox Church, contemporary with the work of Sāwīrus ibn al-Muqaffa. The text bears witness to the place of martyrdom in the self-understanding of Coptic Orthodox Christians, and is an example of a literature that contributes to Coptic Orthodox identity by drawing the sharpest possible lines between Copts and Muslims; for example, Jirjis' tormentors are regularly described as munāfiqīn (hypocrites) and ashrār (evil). In the Ethiopic recension, at least, the story draws sharp lines as well between the 'orthodox' Copts and the Melkites who 'do not truly believe in baptism'

The Role Of The Martyr's Wife

It is clear from the Synaxarion entry that Muzāhim's Christian wife had a role to play in his story: she urged him to seek baptism, fled with him from place to place, and encouraged and strengthened him in his final passion. Despite this role, however, the Synaxarion leaves her nameless. She is simply "a Christian woman" and the saint's wife. We learn much more about Muzāim's wife in the Martyrdom. In the first place, she has a name, written Saywālā in the Coptic Museum manuscript. Even more importantly, she has a major role to play in the text's narrative—Saywālā suffered for her husband's sake: according to the Martyrdom, she was arrested and flogged on no fewer than four occasions. As we have already seen, it was she who pointed out the deficiencies in Muzāim's auto-baptism; it was she who initially gave the interpretation of the vision in which her husband, now known as Jirjis, was called to martyrdom. She supported her husband through his final trials, exhorting him and even, on one occasion when he had been giving scraps of his blood- and pus-soaked bandages to visitors, rebuking him lest he become proud of his baraka-dispensing status. After his death, she received relics of her husband and set up in her home what was, in effect, the first shrine to the martyr. This kind of role is quite unusual in the literature of Christian martyrs of the early Islamic period. These martyrs normally met their destiny alone, humanly speaking (although some received encouragement from heavenly visitors). In contrast to this, Jirjis (Muzāim) is by no means alone, and by no means the sole hero of his Martyrdom. He does have more than his share of heavenly visitors: according to the Martyrdom, the Archangel Michael plays a major role in watching over and healing the saint. Still, the reader cannot overlook the fact that the saint's wife Saywālā has a crucial part to play in the Martyrdom's plot; in fact, she often provides the conviction and steadfastness that sometimes seem to be lacking in the martyr himself. Jirjis' martyrdom, one might say, was a team effort. Just so, the text of the Martyrdom provides models of both male and female steadfastness to its Coptic Orthodox audiences, men and women[5].

George in the Coptic Liturgy:

The Manuscript Paris Copte 23 containing the Interpretations of the Theotokias of the Patriarch Ibn Qiddis (John the 80th patriarch 1300-1320AD) at the end there is a psali for the memento sanctorum (Magma')[6] f.44 a

ΓΕШΡΓΙΟC ΠΑΓΑΡΕΝΝΕΟC   ϢΝΑ2ϯ ΜΠΕϥΙШΤ Αϥ ΧΑϥ

Αϥ ΝΑ2ϯ ΜϢΡΑΝΜΠΧ̅C̅   Αϥ ϢШΠΙ ΜΜΕΝΡΙΤ ΝΤΑϥ

---

5 Mark N. Swanson, "Martyrdom of Jirjis (Muzāhim)," Christian Muslim Relations A bibliographical history, vol. 2 (900-1050), D. Thomas and A. Mallett, (eds), History of Christian-Muslim Relations volume 14, Leiden-Boston: Brill 2010, p 461-62

6 For this book cf. Youhanna Nessim Youssef, Interpretations of the Theotokias by the Patriarch John Ibn Qiddis, Gorgias Eastern Christian Studies 53, New Jersey: Gorgias Press 2020

George the Hagarian, left the faith of his father

He believed in the name of Christ and became His beloved.

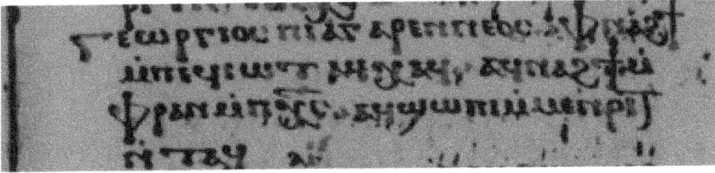

THE MARTYRDOM OF
ST GEORGE MUZAHIM

INTRODUCTION

In the name of the Father, the Son and the Holy Spirit, One God

We begin with the help of God and His success, to explain the martyrdom of the blessed happy saint George the second whose name was before Muzahim.

He attended three assemblies and councils of war. He was greatly tortured and accomplished his martyrdom on the 19th of the month Baūnah in the peace of the Lord Amen.

I inform you my brethren and my beloved about what our Lord Jesus Christ said in His Holy Gospel saying: "Then shall the righteous shine forth as the sun in the kingdom of their Father."[7]

Early Life Of The Saint

Truly this statement was accomplished by you O martyr saint George the second, as he shone as the precious pearl in the dark place. This martyr that we commemorate today was firstly from the race of the Muslim from the sons of Hagar in the district known as Dawritin to the East of Nikiu known as the muddy land to the west of Demeirah Qibly (South) from the county of Sammanud. His father's name was Gami' al-'Sawi from Bani Malh and he married a Christian woman her name was Mariam. He forced her to marry him for she was the fiancée to her cousin, who was a deacon— So he (Gami' al-'Sawi) got from her six sons and one daughter. This saint was the third among them.

His name was Muzahim. When he was brought up and became 12-year-old, he used to meditate his mother going to the feasts of the Christians His relatives -from his mother side- used to

---

7 Mt 13:43.

invite him for the banquet of their feasts. He used to go with them and appreciate Christians when he saw them wearing the splendid garments and going to the church to partake to the communion. When they returned to their houses, he saw their faces joyful by the Holy Spirit, and the odour of their mouths were excellent. When he used to see them in this state, he became greatly jealous. And he used to ask saying: "My lord Jesus Christ have pity upon my poverty and do not Let me die like my father but make me worthy to be baptised with the water of Baptism and to partake Your holy Body and after that I die for your faith."

He used to beseech that night and day. When it was the feast of the pure Lady Mistress Mary On the 21st of the month of Babah [8] he saw group of Christians wearing their best garments and going to the church for celebrating the (feast) of our Lady Saint Mistress Mary, the mother of our Lord Jesus Christ. He swore saying: "By the life of the Lord, I will not taste anything except Until my mother return from the church perhaps I may find something with her from the Oblation (Qurban) to eat it and know what it tastes, and what is it."

First Contact With Christianity

At that time, his friends came to invite him for a banquet as usual, so he said to them: "I cannot eat anything for the time being as I had a medicament, but in the afternoon, I will come to you." As he excused himself, they went and left him. So, he went, purified himself with water and wore his best garment and took his sword on his right hand and walked with the people. He used to look as the group which are in the front of the church's door, where the congregation partook the holy mysteries and

---

8 As the first letters are not clear it could also Tubah

dismissed to their houses. On the spot, he followed his mother until she reached the house and he said to her: "I adjure you, O my mother, by the place where you have come out to give me what you brought with you," pointing to the oblation (Qorban) "to eat it." She said to him: "My son, by your life, no one is able to eat from it except that he takes three hands of water so we can give our oblation and we are neither allowed to talk outsiders about our faith in our Lord Jesus Christ nor about our Lady, according to your faith.

His demand was not heard. Then, he looked to her garments which she wore and saw a little bit of the bread. So, he said to her: "What is this?" she said to him: "This what is left from the bread in the church." So, he stood and took it from the bread against her will and put it in his mouth. As soon as he tasted and found it sweet as sweet as honey. On the spot, the boy was amazed, and he was stupefied for a while. So, he went up to his mother and she said: "What happened to you, why you came up to me in such manner!" He said to her: "My mother, the piece of bread that I took from you against your will, became in my mouth like honey." When his mother heard from this, she was extremely amazed and she said: "My son, since long time, since my childhood till now I partake from the oblations in the church. And this amazing mystery was never revealed to me; but I ask you my son, do not inform anybody about this mystery because if your father knows this, he will kill you."

Decision To Become Christian

From this day, he put in his heart to become Christian. When his deeds became apparent to his father, he said to him: "I swear by God, if you do not finish the acts of the Christians, I will kill you in the evilest way. When the Lord Jesus Christ wished to attract him this martyr George the second through as

Christian woman her name was Mariam, and she was Melkite. So, he revealed his secret and said to her that he wanted to be Christian. So, she said to him: "If you want to become a true Christian come with me as if I want to visit my family and when we will arrive at that place, I will invite them to baptize you." When he heard this from her, he arose and went with her to a town called Barbayah from the district of the city of Damietta. She took him to a priest who was a relative to her mother and she informed him about his state. He said to her: "Be patient and tomorrow as it is the feast of the angel Michael, we will baptize infants so we will baptize him with them." In the next day, he went and bathed and wore his clothes and went to the church. While the priest was baptising in the baptistery the devil pushed a Muslim woman, possessed by an evil spirit, she came in the middle of the church and fall down and cried out saying: "O men from Barbayah , behold among you in the church a Muslim man from the sons of Haggar and he wants to be baptised, so if you baptise him it will be the destruction of your town because of him, and this church will be demolished, and the all the priests will be killed." When the priest heard these sayings, he put him out of the church fearing to baptise him. The saint was extremely sad and he did not eat anything on that day. In the next day, he stood and prayed as it was his custom. The angel of the Lord, crowned with lights, appeared to him and said to him: "Do not be sad, for they did not baptise you in this place as they are not orthodox and they do not confess the straight faith of the baptism, but arise and go to our father the bishop Anba Zacharias in the harbour of Damietta."

The First Attempt For Baptism

So, he arose and went to go there, he was hosted by an elder man, whose name John (Yuhanna). He informed him about his secret and the elder said to him: "My son be aware not to inform the bishop that you are Hanafite so he would expel you from baptism and he will not wish to baptise, but tell him, that polluted your body with a Muslim woman, for he is afraid from the inhabitants of the city as they hate the Christian and they do not baptise except on the 21st of Baunah which is the feast of the Lady, the mother of Salvation. So, he dwelt with this elder until the feast of the Lady and he went to the church to the father Zacharias the bishop. He found them as they prepared the baptistry, so the saint advanced to the father, bishop and kissed his hands and said to him as the elder John, who hosted him, told him. The bishop told him: "My son, a man cannot be baptised twice, but I will order the priest to fill (basin) with water and to up it under the altar till I finish the liturgy and after that they will bring it and read the prayers that suit your case and I will pour on you and I believe that you will be purified from the sin that you committed but be aware not to do it another time." So, the saint swore by the elevated God while he was in the hands of the bishop that he will not do it again, but he will comfort his heart. There was an elder priest standing next to the baptistery, so the martyr advanced and kissed his hands saying: "I adjure you by the Lord, O holy father, on this great day Which is the day of the Lady, the mother of Salvation when you finish baptizing the kids, do not release the water, until the congregation is dismissed from the church, and you will take the opportunity to baptise me." So, the priest as the saint told him and kept the water for him.

The Baptism Of The Saint

When the congregation went out of the church, the saint descended into the water and deepened himself three time in the name of the Holy Trinity, the Father, the Son and the Holy

Spirit and he took his clothes, and the priest gave him from the holy mysteries (sacraments) and dismissed him in peace. He went from him, and he was happy. The next day, the 22nd of Baunah, he found a boat travelling to Dimeirah. So, he took it and went to his town. It happened that the priest from the Northern Basut, whose name was Abanub, but he left it and went to Al-Dawrutin. The priest had a virgin daughter, and she was perfect, as she was raised in the house of her father. She used to obey God, night and day and her name was Saywālā, when the martyr saw her, God put her love in his heart until he married her after the betrothal and the pure marriage. When she spent some time with him. She asked him how he became Christian. So he informed her from the beginning to the end and what he did in Damietta. When she heard from him these words, she became sad, and said to him: "What you are[not baptised till now as I see from my father, with my own eyes that if they want to baptise kids they should bring them first to the church and the priest will read a prayer then the priest will anoint on their faces till they are purified and then they confess the suitable confession and after that the priest anoint them with the oil of Galileon and introduce them to the baptistery font and baptise them. After the baptism he anoint them with the holy Myron and upon this they are considered among the Christian congregation. As for you, you did not do anything of this, but if you obey me and follow me, you come with me to my town, and I will let them to baptise you and you will become a perfect Christian." When he heard these words, he was extremely rejoiced. While they were thinking about this matter and preparing it, the cursed devil excited some evil people si they went to the military commander in Demeira at that time whose name Raddad ibn Madi and he was Hanafite and they calumniated the saint saying: "This man belonged to our religion and on these days he became Christian." When he heard this statement, it became very difficult to him and on the spot and rode his horse and followed by his servants and soldiers and came to Al-Dawrutin and planted his tents outside the village and sent his servants to the house of the saint. They bound and took him and brought him to him (the military commander). This is the first martyrdom of George the second confessed in front of the Raddad ibn Madi, the governor, in the peace of the Lord Amen!

First Interrogatory, And Torture

When they bound from his hands, he said to him: "Are you Muzahim al-'Asawi ibn Gami'." He said to him: "yes" The military commander said to him: "Why you left the religion of your father, and you became Christian." The saint replied and said to him: "I am Christian openly and I am the servant of the Lord Jesus Christ, the Son of the Living God. I am not a thief or killer but because of the name of my Lord Jesus Christ's sake, I was delivered to you and whatever you want to do it."

When he heard this word from him, he became extremely angry and order to put him on his chest, and to torture him with all sorts of tortures so that his blood was shedding like running water and afterwards he ordered him to return to his house and to take all what is inside and to give to 70 evil servants. He said to them: "Take this falling apart person and throw him in prison and do not feet or give him to drink till he dies. Then, throw his in the sea."

The Saint And His Wife Left The Town

While they were walking with him till, they reached the bridge of Al-Dawrutin, and there was a voice crying in the desert: "O servants return this man to the emir." On the spot, they returned to him. The governor said to them: "Why you returned him to me." So, the servants told him: "You sent to us to return him and that is why we returned him, and we cannot object." So, he said to them: "I did not send to return him." They informed what happened and the governor was amazed of what took place. While the saint was standing between his hands, the angel of the Lord came to him as a notable (archon) man and [took] the saint and delivered him from their [hands]

When he returned to his house, he said to his wife: "My sister we cannot stay in this place, for these evil people know us and they have power over us, let us go to a place where we are not known and do what God plans for us. And we will live with our Lord and Saviour Jesus Christ, that I believed in him who will manage our affairs wherever we are."

Accusation Of Hamdan

While they were thinking that (matter) an evil man from the inhabitant of Nikiu his name is Hamdan advanced to the military commander and said: "What did you do for us these evil deeds as you left this Christianised who put in shame our religion and followed another one, so if he would not return to our religion, I will kill him." On the spot, he gave him his servant and walked in front of them and took them to the house of the saint. They found him sitting with his wife thinking what they wanted to do. They wanted to bound him, so the saint came out to them. They were unable to take him as the Lord delivered him from their hands. They followed to catch him, but they were unable to do it, so they caught his wife Saywālā, took her out and bitted her with fifty times with palm branches till her blood flowed on earth. They took what was left from the plunder of the house, they bound to a tail of horse and turned around the whole town. No one was able to deliver her from his hands and afterwards, he took her out of Al-Dawrutin, and he wanted to take her to the city of Nikiu, behold, a lady called Christa, a wife of a man-deacon, called Yasîb. She went to a priest called Mercurius and she said: "I asked to go with me to this evil man and to be the sponsor of this woman to deliver her from his hands." Therefore, the saint (the priest) came out with the lady and sponsored the wife of the saint and delivered her from his hands.

The next day, Hamadan came to Al-Dawrutin and order to bring the woman to his hands. He said to her: "Do you know where your husband is?" She said: "I do not know where he is." So, he repeated the question and adjured her, that if she wanted the return of her husband she will die by death. Few days later, the saint returned to the south of Al-Dawrutin and he was hiding in the dwelling of some of his friends. They brought her to him. He said: "I was informed, my sister that you received harsh tortures for my sake. So, if you want to leave me, what you say?"

The Saint Wished To Become A Monk And His Wife Objected

She said: "By the Living Lord, my Lord Jesus Christ, even if I shed my blood for you, I will never leave you till the day of my death. For [I am ready] to die for the name of our Lord Jesus Christ's sake." When he heard this statement from her: "He thanked God." And said to her: "Be fortified, my sister in the Lord, you will receive the wage of your pains, as for me, I will go to the south so if the Lord makes my way successful to find a good place, I will come to take you." When he said these words, he went away from her, so she returned to her house. On the next day, the devil took the form of an old man from the Muslim of the town and preached saying: "Do you know that Muzahim arrived tonight to here, he wanted to return to the religion of his fathers, but his wife came to him and encouraged him till his heart inclined to the religion of the Christians and as we heard she sent him to the monastery of Abba Maqar (Saint Macarius monastery) to become monk." When they heard this, they wished to take her. She fled and hid herself.

Arrestation Of His Wife

An evil woman came to them and informed where she is. So, on the spot, they came and gave her sound beating and took her to Demeira to Raddad the military commander to kill her. The Lord gave her grace in front of him, so, asked the Christian notables to deliver her from the hands of the evil men. When the saint heard what happened to her as tortures, so he secretly came to her and took her to the south.

The Saint Fled To The South And Another Slander

He dwelt in a hamlet called Soft where he found wherein a found a good way to live. He spent some days there, but the devil when he saw him praying to the Lord Jesus Day and night without cease to mention Him. A boy from the inhabitants of Nikiu who knew very well the saint, so he entered to the place wherein the saint was working which was oil press and started to inform the workers about all what happened to the saint. When the saint found that his secret was revealed to the people, went to his house, and informed his wife saying to her: "Today, I find a boy from the inhabitant of Nikiu, when he knows me, I verified that he started to inform people about my case."

Tortures In Mahalah Ruh

He did not finish his talk with her, that the mentioned boy followed him to his house with a large group of Muslim holding swards and weapons they held the saint without mercy, and they put a cord around his neck and pulled him to the streets of the town. They tortured him with all kinds of tortures. And man among the people came from behind him and hit with his sward on his heard, to make into. The saint fall down on his face. The news reached as far as the city of al-Mahallah to Abu al-Abašîr ibn Satua that a man killed, a worker from you press, so, he arose and rode his animal and took with him some of his friends and came to Soft al-Qudur and delivered him from them and freed him. He said with guile: "Stay here and do not be afraid and remain in your work, wishing in himself to give him a delay until Friday to take him to the Mosque and if he would not pray with the people, he would burn him alive. There was among the workers of the press, a Christian man, whose name was Maqarah when he knew their intention and what they wanted to do with the saint, he hastily came to the saint and told him: "Why are you in this place, arise and free yourself on the spot if not you will save yourself and many tribulations will come upon you from the evil men." So, he arose with his wife and went out this village on Wednesday the 29th of Baramhat, which is the feast of the annunciation, they were fasting on that day. They walked towards Mahalat Ruh on the first part of the night. When they did not find a boat to cross (the river), they entered into the thorns and spines; and spent there the night to the morning> The morrow they crossed (the river) and came to a district called Siriyah and they spent there seven days. Then they went to a place called Tantatah and dwelt there for three years, while they were safe. The devil could not stand this so he stirred some people from the inhabitants of the district and they said: "You look a [Muslim] man." He replied to them: "I am

Christian from father to grand-father." However, these people intended to torture him. He took his wife and travelled to a district called Akhna. He dwelt there for three years.

Finally, The Canonical Baptism Of The Saint

So, the devil- the enemy of the humankind- brought a severe illness. He used to thank the Lord night and day, his wife used to fortify him in his faith and encourage him and to say: "My brother, how many times the devil tempted you and the Lord Jesus Christ saved you from all of them. I see you sick and I do not know what will happen to you, I am worried, as you were not baptised with the Baptism of Lord Jesus Christ. So, in order to enjoy life with you, please obey me, let us go to the church and I will baptise you a perfect Baptism as it should be for Christians. If we live so we live for the Lord." The saint had a friend in Mahalat Khalaf from Sammanud county, called Theodorus, who was a guardian. They arose on the spot and went to him and informed him about their secret. He was very happy. He took them to a Christian priest called Abba Amun and his brother was the leader of the deacons called Yuannis (John). So, when he informed them about the case of the saint, they were extremely happy and order the holy bread maker to prepare for them. When it was the time of the liturgy, they went to the church, they made him to stand in front of the altar and the priest read the prayer which is the beginning of the baptism. Then they went to the Jordan (the baptistery font) and baptised the saint in the name of the Father, the Son and the Holy Spirit and they celebrated (the mass) in the sanctuary and gave the holy communion to him and he (the priest) dismissed them in peace. Theodorus took them to his house and made a banquet. In this place, he changed his name from Muzahim to Girgis (George) after saint George the Palestinian. On the morrow, they arose and went to the district of al-Difhawiyah called the house of Gimianah.

Ascetical Practices Of The Couple

They spent there three years. The saint made an agreement in the Lord with his wife not to touch her and make their bed pure, without blame to the day of their death. This what happened with them, keeping purity and prayer night and day because without purity no one can see the Lord. They used to remain in the church during the time of prayers and liturgies. All what they earned they gave as alms for the poor, the needy. It happened on the 17th of Abib which was a Saturday they came out of the house of Gimianah and went to Asbut the town of his wife and they dwelt there. She took him to the house of her father, so they dwelt in it. He used to stay in the church lighting the candles and serving well. He used to make secret prayers, doing 500 prostrations (metanias) every night. The Lord was please of his deeds. When the Lord wished to call him for the invitation of martyrdom. While he was thinking in his heart saying: "Why am I here and the devil is tempting with temptations, I will go to the monastery of saint Macarius and be a monk there till the day of my death." While he was thinking about 1that, he saw a vision as if he ascended to heaven and they made him to sit on the right of the Lord Jesus Christ and he heard as voice saying: "Be strong George (Girgis) in the martyrdom, blessed are you as you became worthy to be counted with the martyrs, the saints and to receive the heavenly crown with the just in the Kingdom of the Lord Jesus Christ. Do not be afraid of George (Girgis), the pains are little, and the graces are numerous. When he saw this (vision), his strength increased, and he informed his wife about that. When his wife heard this statement, she said to him: "As you see in this vision, the Lord does not want you to become monk, but He wants to reveal His Holy Name and to receive the imperishable crown of martyrdom, and the great joy and I will be called the wife of a martyr." She was rejoicing and happy in front of him, strengthening his heart of the struggle for the martyrdom. When the martyr heard the speech of his wife, he went to a religious priest- monk, he was a wise scribe and he said: "My holy father, I wish to go to the monastery of Abba Macarius to become monks however I am afraid that the Lord will be angry against me as I did not reveal His Name on Earth in front of people and die for His Holy Name's sake." The monk said to him: "You know better your situation, my son. If you fear torture, go to the monastery of Abba Macarius and be monk. If not, they will take council against you to arrest you by the governor of this district, as I heard. But blessed are you my son George, if you endure one punishment is better that your stay in monastery a whole year." When he heard these words, he went to his house and informed his wife. She used to strengthen him saying: 'My lord and brother, I did not cease to tell you if you endure, you will be blessed from God.' From that day, he was prepared and started to be seen openly. So now, O beloved Christian brethren who are attending this feast I wish to show to you what the Lord revealed to this martyr before he started his struggle for the martyrdom. When it was the 22nd of Bašans, it was a Thursday, while he was thinking in his heart, whether I will be able to endure such torture or not but let the Will of God be done. He thanked the Lord and he saw (a dream) as if he was present in a council of the military commander with a [group] of martyrs like and they were tortured with all sorts of torture, and they did not feel anything as if they accomplished their martyrdom in their bodies. Lord Jesus Christ was resurrecting them from death. When he saw this wonderful vision, he became extremely happy and knew that the Lord will help him, so he fell on his face. He slept and saw also An Angel of the Lord crowned with lights saying: "Be strong George so for he that shall endure unto the end, the same shall be saved. [9] Because of this saying I prepared you to die for the name of our Lord Jesus Christ's sake." The next day, he went to the church cleaning it and lighting its lamps and he stood to pray with the congregation. When the Holy Gospel was read as chapter from Matthew saying: "Behold, I send you forth as sheep in the midst of wolves: be ye therefore wise as serpents, and harmless as doves."[10] And the rest of the chapter. Then, they celebrated the liturgy (Quddas) and the Gospel of Luke was read saying: "And I say unto you my friends, Be not afraid of them that kill the body, and after that have no more that they can do. But I will forewarn you whom ye shall fear: Fear him, which after he hath killed hath power to cast into hell; yea, I say unto you, Fear him."[11] When the saint heard these sayings full of life and meditated in his heart, and became aware that this could happen, so he remained silent till the end of the liturgy. He went to his house and said to his wife: "My sister! Let us eat some bread as I do not know what will happen today." So, she hasted to prepare the table and they ate together, and she was strengthening his faith saying: "Be strong my brother so if you endure a little bit the torture, you will receive numerous graces in the Heavenly Kingdom forever Amen."

---

9 Mat 24: 13.

10 Mat 10:16

11 Luke 12: 4-5 (Mat 10:28)

The Second Martyrdom In Demeira In The Reign Of Baraz Ibn Sulayman[12]

He arose on the spot and prepared his riding animal and went out of his house. He arrived at a close district called Mima to take a little bit of wheat to bring to his house. There was in Demeira an evil man called Ubaid and he was among the leaders with the military commander, he went to a group of evil men and informed them about the story of the saint saying: "Behold, there is a man from Absut who a Muslim was and became Christian and left the religion of Islam, so if we leave him, he will be an authority and will corrupt the hearts of people of the Muslim and make them Christians." When the evil (men) heard his statement, they ordered to bring him to them. On the spot, he took two from the servants of the military commander and went to the saint's house seeking him and they did not find him. They said to his wife: "Where is your husband." She said: "I do not know his place." So, and they expelled her out of the district.

They were seeking the saint everywhere. So, some evil people informed them that he went to Mima for a special matter. They hasted to seek him, by the will of the Lord, they found him in the way walking after his riding animal loaded with wheat. It was the seventh hour of the day which was the 23rd of Bašans, it was a Saturday. When the evil man Ubayd saw him, he said to him: "O George, we went to your house, this hour, seeking you, and we did not find you." The saint advanced wishing to kiss his hand (of Ubayd) so he stretched his hand and took his

---

12 This Is The Second Martyrdom In Demeira In The Reign Of Baraz Ibn Sulayman, May The Prayers Of The Saint Be With All Of Us Amen!

turban and put it around his neck, the servants turned around his shoulder beating him brutally and took him riding animal with all its load and the cloth that he was wearing, and they put a cord around his neck, they went to Demeira. When they entered to the city, they took him to the house of the deputy whose name was Bašîr al-Afrangi (the Frank) so, he ordered to throw the saint in a dark cell. They closed the door. The saint stood up in the night to pray until the sun of the 24th of Bašans rose, which is the feast of the coming of the Lord Christ to the Land of Egypt. The cursed devil, took the shape of a man and wandered in the streets of the city saying: "This man that you are waiting for, was locked to the deputy." So, many evil men gathered to him as those who met Pilate. When he took him out from the place where he was, they tortured him with all sorts of tortures: some of them spitted on his face, some were beating mercilessly him on his head, some of them were beating his neck, and his shoulders with iron pins till they broke his bones. The saint was enduring all these tortures, meditating with ceasing the Lord Jesus Christ while he was in the midst of them bound with a wooden beam in his hands and feet. His hands were put in the back. He was happy and joyful, and he did not feel anything of the torture.

When the news reached the military commander in Demeira, whose name was Baraz Ibn Sulayman, on the spot, he sent strong servants and took him (the saint).

When he stood between his hands (Baraz), he told him: "Woe to you, why did you leave the religion of your fathers and followed the religion of the Christians. Now you are worthy of great torture, but we will honour your so you may return to your previous religion." There was in the council the judge of the district and another man called Sulayman ibn ʿabd al-Hamid, a very clever Moroccan man. This Moroccan was the executioner of Maš'alah the military commander of the city of

Tannis and large group of soldiers who were taking the same discourse to the martyr so that he returned to the religion of Islam saying: "What will you win to leave your religion and follow the religion of the Christians? They do not appreciate your value. You are tortured everywhere because of that. Long life to our lord Baraz if you listen and obey and return to the religion of your father, we will give you gold, and silver and garments and all your needs forever." The martyr replied to them saying: "By my Lord Jesus Christ if you give me all the kingdoms of Baraz, I will not listen to you. Do you want me to be like Judah Ischariot who sold his master for 30 Dirhams? But Live be to the Lord Jesus Christ if you give me all what you have, I will not deny my Lord Jesus Christ."

When the judge heard that he insulted the saint and hastily he spitted on his face and punched his mouth as the Jews did for the Lord. According to what is written in the Holy Gospels, 'The disciple is not above [his] master, nor the servant above his lord.' [13] They were torturing him from early morning of Sunday to the sixth hour. When they found that he did not obey them. They said to each other: "We will not kill him here so that would not please of 'Adî ibn Harb the military commander of these districts but we will send him (the saint) to him (('Adî) to do whatever he wants.'

The Third Martyrdom In The Reign Of Baraz

On the spot, they took him out of the prison, and they made him cross the river to the South- Demeira, where 'Adî, the military commander was there in charge of the districts. They did not find him, they searched for him, and they were informed that he is with the bishop Anba Maqarah in his cell as he prepared a

---

13 Mat 10:24

banquet for him on that day. They took the saint to the North-Demeira to Baraz the governor. Baraz repeated the same speech to leave what he is doing by holding the religion of Christ. He did not accept from him. The abovementioned Moroccan was the executioner was ready to prepare a harsh torture for the saint among these he took a palm fibres cord around his neck and bound to the mast of the boat while the face of the saint was towards the mast and the fibre palm cord around him from his head up to his feet. Then the military commander told him: "turn your face to see you" On the sport the mighty Moroccan jumped and hold the head of the saint and turned behind so that all the nerves of his neck cracked and all who were present heard this. Then, he tortured him till their reached Mira the south, so he ordered to loosen him from the mast and to lock him in the bath of al-Mawsili as it was close to the rise. He ordered the herald to ring the bell in the city saying: "Come o people to see this man who left the religion of his father and followed the religion of the Christians and was baptised with their baptism and partook the communion. He entirely joined them, and worshiped Jesus' son of Mary and he took him as God, and now I harshly torture him to see how His God can save him from my hands." Upon this 'Adî looked, the military commander at him saying: "What do you say? Return to your religion or if not, I will harshly torture you that the previous one will not be considered as something." The blessed replied to him saying: "What do you want to hear from me? My life is My Lord Jesus Christ the Son of the Living God. If you give me all your belonging or if you torture me for the whole year, I will not deny the name of my Lord Jesus Christ." On the spot, he ordered to hang him on the easel flagging him with whips by two in front of him and two behind him from the seventh hour up to the sunset, then to beat him with iron chains that are used for horses. He was enduring all those as if he was not harmed, he never ceased to mention Jesus Christ during all his tortures.

Some stablemen servants took the wooden rod from the stable and came behind him to beat him on his head and make it into two.

'Adî, the military commander, had a Christian wife that he much esteemed her, for she was the daughter of the notable Marut, and he took her against his will. She was very pretty. When she saw the tortures that they tortured the saint, she sent to the military commander saying: "Swear by the life of the sultan, do not let these evildoer people to kill this just man, so you will oversee his offense; but throw him in the prison until you consult your father of his case and whatever is his reply obey. Lest you kill this man and not to inform him, so he will blame you for that." When he heard this from his wife, he put aside the saint who was about to die. Four men carried him and threw him in a house to the East of the residence of the governor. They put a huge beam on his leg> They assigned a barbarian man, whose name was Salman, one of the evilest servants. When it was midnight, the Angel of the Lord Michael appeared to him saying: "Be strong, and do not fear for there is little pains and the repose is numerous." He wiped by his hands the body of the saint and healed him from all his wounds. He ascended to heaven while he was watching him- as testified to us a Christian monk from the monastery of saint Macarius named Mina, as he was imprisoned with the saint.

The Saint In Prison - Heavenly Appiration

He (the monk) said, when the saint was thrown in the prison, a pious Christian woman, called Damianah, entered to him, as her house was next to the prison and she had a vessel full of oil, she emptied on the wounds of his head. She saw as if the oil was going out of the ears of the saint from the strength of the wound that was in his head. Then the saint reposed on the eleventh hour of the night and the Pure Chaste, Mistress Mary, the mother of the salvation appeared to him like a white dove and spread her wing over the head of the saint and put her beak in the wounds of his head and awoke him from his sleep. He lifted his head and held her right wing, so she flied from his hand and went out the door of the prison.

She was very luminous. He put his hand on the place of his wound and he found that it was cured, and his body became very strong, nothing was hurting him. The next day, which is the third day of the saint's imprisonment, as he did not eat or drink, his wife Saywālā came to visit him and to fortify him. She found him cured from all his pains, and when she looked at him, she found him determined. She said: "My brother and my lord, the matter that the evil people brought upon you, three days ago and I heard when they arrested you from the road of Mima and they did not forgive you from torture and they came early on Sunday and continued to torture you till the sunset and broke your hands and legs and all your members. They turned your neck to break it and divided your head. But now I thank Lord Jesus Christ that I did not find anything which were mentioned about you. I see you standing with beauty and strength." When the saint heard the speech of his wife, he smiled with the Holy Spirit and said: "My sister, all they mentioned about me is true, but I thank my Lord Jesus Christ who sent me his angel and healed my whole body. While the Pure chaste, the Mother of Salvation, Mistress Mary appeared to me like a white dove and healed me from all my pains. Let the Lord Live, my sister, if the Christians know the strength and the proof

I would deliver myself to torture and death since the time that I entered in this religion, but this is the day that the will of God to reveal His Name. My sister, pray to the Lord and remember me that He may help me to accomplish the martyrdom." She answered him saying: "My brother, know the value of this grace and the favour and the honour that you received because of the Lord's sake. And if you endure you will get the sublime honour and your name will be mentioned for the coming generation." When they finished talking with each other, she went out from him, she was happy. It was midnight the saint stood to pray and beseech from the Lord as his custom. The Angel of the Lord Michael appeared to him, and his light enlightened the who prison, and a great fire fall so that they thought that the entire city was burned because of the greatness of the light. The military commander jumped as he thought that the granary burned. He sent his servants to inquire about the truth of the matter. They returned to him saying there is nothing happened. So, his wife replied to him saying: "the fire that you saw is not a fine from the world, but it clearly appeared on the prison to help this just imprisoned man for the name of the Lord Jesus Christ's sake." When he heard this speech, he was amazed. The next day he ordered that no one should visit the saint in prison as for some faithful used to visit him every day to see his matters in the Lord. There was with the saint as Christian man from the inhabitants of city of Nigal, whose name was Mina, he was very sad, and sorrowful because of the agriculture taxes (Kharag) and he was unable to pay anything. The saint called him saying: "My brother Mina, I see you sad and sorrowful behold your family visits you and will sponsor your debts and make you go out of the prison." Even before finishing his dialogue with the saint, the family of Mina came and sponsored him and took him out, and the discourse of the saint was accomplished. When it was the 28th of Bašans, a monk called Severus came to him and greeted him and kissed him and said: "Be strong my brother and do not be afraid, because day before yesterday I passed to the East of Damietta and I found the servants of the military commander pulling a just layman called Abu al-Kheir and torturing him of the Lord Jesus Christ's sake, when I drew near him he said to me: 'My father Severus if you go to Demeira go to my brother George and ask about him. Tell him to be strong and do not fear as I heard your news that you were tortured for Christ's sake and I wished, me the unworthy from the Lord to reach my desire. I saw the Angel of the Lord, with three crowns of luminous diamond. I said what are these luminous crowns. He said to me: 'These luminous crowns that you saw in my hand are prepared for George who is tortured in Demeira for the name of Lord Christ's sake. And now my brother asks about him and tell him be strong as he will meet Christ before me, if the Lord helps you to achieve your martyrdom, remember me to the Lord, that we may gather you and me in the heavenly kingdom with joy.' When the saint heard this speech from the monk, he praised the Lord. Me, the wretched poor humble the unworthy to be called deacon from the inhabitants of Biala, I heard about this saint that he was imprisoned in the south of Demeira for the Lord Christ's sake, and I desired to come to him and visit him for the Lord's sake. I had a relative called Julius, he was a priest, and his foot was wounded that was very painful, when he knew that I would go to the saint, he adjured me by the name of Christ to come with him to the saint and to get his blessings. On the spot, we searched for a riding animal, but we did not find, so, I wanted to leave him and to go but because of the strength of his faith, he said to me: 'even if I die on the road, it is imperative for me to go to this saint and get his blessing, perhaps I will get joy through him.' I walked slowly, slowly as his foot was exceedingly hurting him, till we reached to the place the place was. When we got his blessings and we were about to go, he held the hand of the saint and put on his painful foot and prayed on it. On the spot, his food was cured, and we came out from him, glorifying God. The next day, it was a Wednesday, a group of the employers who were Baraz and Bašîr al-Afrangi and the slaves, and all the leaders and went to 'Adî the military commander saying: "Deliver to us this man so we kill him." He replied saying: "I cannot deliver to you until

I receive a letter from my father in the city of Tannis." When they became angry and insisted in their demand for the group who was present. He swore by the life of Baraz that he will not deliver him to them. So they went from him very angry. He used to increase praying to the eve of Sunday. While he was praying, he heard a voice saying: "George be strong and do not fear." The saint was happy and rejoicing from that day till the 12th of Baunah while he was standing praying, he heard a voice from heaven and a bell and a herald says: 'come and see this new miracle that happens these days as there is nothing similar in the ancient times.' He said, I also saw a numerous group following this herald and I also followed him till reached to the west of Demeira where there was a demolished church named after the angel Michael and the church named after Abba Nofer toward the palm tree next to the springs (? Muballat) and the herald stopped on that place I stood next to him, and the herald said to me with a loud voice: 'Be strong, O George, this is the place where you will accomplish your martyrdom.' When he said this to me. I awoke from my sleeping. The police were coming with the servants of the military commander, they were freighting him some of them said tomorrow we will burn you alive and other said we will hang a millstone were about your neck, and [that] we will drown in the depth of the sea [14] and others said to him: 'we need to hang you on the palm tree, that I saw in the vision.

Then his wife entered to him, so, he repeated all that, so she comforted him saying: "Be strong, my brother, do not fear and do not be frightened from these sayings, by your life my brother, when I heard these about you, I stood, last night and I did neither eat nor drink and I saw in the dream a voice saying to me: ' why your hear is frightened, O Saywālā, for your husband,

---

14 Mat 18:6

go to him and let him know to strengthen himself and his will as he will not be killed unless the Lord permits." When she talked to him with this speech, she went out from him.

When it was the 8th of Baunah, and it was a Sunday, on the sixth hour of the day, during the time of oblation, the saint saw three crowned men with light entered to him. One stood on his right and another on his left and one in front of him. As for the one in front of him, he was unable to see Him because of the greatness of His light. The one who was on his right, said: "O George, do you know who am I?" he said: "No, my lord." He said to him: I am Michael the archangel who is standing to the right of God, the one on your left is Gabriel the announcer of life as for the one whom you were unable to see because of the greatness of His light is our Lord, our Saviour Jesus Christ who came to fortify you and to help you, as a bad hour will reach you on this day." When the archangel said this, they ascended to heaven, while he was watching them. The saint was thinking what will happen to me in this hour that the angel mentioned. While he was thinking two barbarians entered to him, they were very evil policemen and they had green palm branches and they made teeth like saw and they said to him with anger: "What do you say You return to the religion of your fathers or not?" He replied to them saying: "I did not cease to say to you that I will never do it." Upon hearing this speech, they became very angry and ordered to put on his right side and both beat in the same place on his thigh till blood shed from his flesh on the palm tree branches, and his nerves of his fore were cut. The saint cried saying:" My Lord, my Saviour, the Son of the living God help me." When those barbarians did this, they went out from his (cell) and left him rolling in the blood. When the news reached his wife that he was beaten in the prison, and she was in the harbour outside of Demeira with a nun, she hasted and came to him in the night. When she saw suffering, she smiled, by the Holy Spirit, and said to him: "Good, my brother, I rejoiced that now you would receive a great honour instead for this little pain." He was unable to reply to her from the pains that he had. She went out, she was sorrowful, crying because of what she saw. She remained that night without eating or drinking but praying to the Lord that He may strengthen him from this torture. The next day, she stood and went to the market to the physicians [15] and took from them ointments that suit wounds. She went to the prison and treated his tight as he was tired and had a sever fever. She said to him: "Rejoice, now, O holy of the Lord, George, why you are weak. I rejoice every day and today the joy is over because you are counted worthy to suffer shame for his name. [16] If you do not endure and thank the Lord, you will not have wage for the Lord Jesus Christ tempted you with this punishment to see your love to Him. Therefore, be strong and do not fear for our Lord Jesus Christ tempted you with this punishment, will cone to heal you. You should be happy and rejoice as much as your tortures multiply, the crowns are prepared to you in the Heavenly Kingdom." When she said these discourses, she went out, she was weeping and hiddenly crying and did not show him this not to weaken his faith and soul. When it was Wednesday 11th of Baunah which is the feast of saint Claudius, the saint was heavily suffering from his thigh because there was swollen, he was beating it and he was asking the Lord saying: "My Lord, my God, Jesus Christ, that I believed in him, through the intercessions of saint Claudius the Martyr, whose feast is today, heal me from this affliction." Upon finishing this in his heart, some servants of the governor entered to him saying: "Today the military commander will kill you." When he heard this, he stood up on and raised his hands to

---

15 Lit. "the hair dressers" at that time the hair dresser was the doctor of the village
16 Acts 5:41

the sky and said: "My Lord, Jesus Christ, You know everything before it happens, You know my love to You because of my pains and my death for Your holy Name (but 1 ask) Your mercy as I relayed upon You, Jesus My life, Jesus my strength, Jesus my hope, Jesus my glory, Jesus my pride, O Lord Jesus Christ hear my prayer, as I cried to you, lest they come tomorrow wanting to take me outside the city wishing to kill me, so I cannot walk, so these infidel swill mock me that his God is unable to heal him and consider you as weak, O who has the power, the might, the kingdom for ages of ages." He was asking the angel of the Lord Michael in some of his prayers. When it was midnight, Michael the archangel entered to him with a white garment like snow[17] and said to him: "Rejoice O servant of Jesus Christ, George, the chosen for me, today is one week since you asked the Lord for you, and he sent to you this garment so it will give you strength. Advance to me so I will clothe you." Then, the saint advanced to him, and he put the cloth on him. It became one with his body and he signed his thigh with the sign of the Cross. On the spot, pus and blood came out of it, and on the spot, he was healed. When it was the 13th of Baunah, some people from the inhabitants of Baltan, Barhatmus to get blessing from him as his fame reached the lands of Egypt. They asked him saying: "We beseech you, O holy of the Lord, to give us blessing from you to our houses." He gave them the bandages which were on his feet and legs which were full of blood. They took with faith and joy and went out in the peace. When his wife heard this, she came to him like Theoclia, and Theognosta, the wife of Evrandius who was blaming the martyrs, also, she said to her husband with anger: "Who are you, o humble, to deserve this fame to be called as martyrs and to give people bandages from your body as blessing. Are you like Peter, John and Paul [18] the

---

17 Apoc 1: 14.
18 Act 5: 15-16

Apostle who used to give his bandage of his body for the sick people, so they were cured, and they put the leprous and they resurrected the death? But you, you became proud in front of the Lord as a martyr, let me know what punish did you get or what affliction did you endure for the name of Christ? Did the worms come out of your body and your legs did you see your nerves cut and thrown in front of you like the previous martyrs? No one of them became proud in front of the God except you! You should avoid them and kiss the feet of those who come to you and ask them to remember you in their prayers. How did you allow them the kiss your head? But, as the Lord lives, if you do it again, I will not come to you, and I will not talk to you till the day of my death." When the saint heard this speech from his wife, he bitterly wept and swore that he would never do it again. She went out of him.

Another Accusation - Tortures

Afterwards, the evil men of the inhabitants of Demeira and went to Abu Lir the brother of the military commander and complained his brother to him saying: "By God, if you do not push your brother to deliver this converted to Christianity to kill him, we will all become Christian by envy!"

So, Abu Lir advanced to his brother 'Adî and said to him: "My brother, deliver this man to them to do as they wish." 'Adî said to his brother: "My brother, I wrote several letters to my father regarding him, and I am waiting his reply. Be patient till Sunday, I will deliver him to you." When they heard this, they left him on the sport. The saint remained in the prison till 15th of Baunah. And there was with 'Adî, a very evil servants of council, and he was full of hatred the saint, he went to a man known as 'Abd-Allah and he was a friend of the in charge of (the town of) Gorgar and he said to him: "If you walk me to the prison and help me to kill his convert and whatever you want I will give you."

They went to the prison and when they entered to the saint, he lifted his leg and kicked the saint in his face. He was wearing high heel so the iron point pierces the face of the saint and made a big wound so that the whole place was covered by blood. He took a hammer of thorns and was beating the saint till he fell down unconscious. There was around the prison many Christians. When they saw what happened to the saint, they shout so the military commander heard them, so he took them (the evil servants) out of the prison. When the Christians entered, they found lying down smeared with blood. They hasted to washing that blood and they sat net to him crying. When he saw them crying, he smiled and said: "My brethren do not cry, Let my Lord Jesus Christ, that I believed in Him, live all what befallen on me, I did not care at all for the power of the Lord was with me in this fourth time since I came here. The first one was for my Lord Jesus Christ, the second was for the archangel Michael, the third one was for the announcer Gabriel, this fourth time is for the Pure chaste Lady, Mistress Mary. Now my brethren, remember me in your prayers so that the Lord helps me to accomplish the martyrdom. As according to the vision, I will accomplish my struggle on the 19th of Baunah which a Thursday." When he said this to them, they went out glorifying God. He wife continued to strengthen his heart every day and to comfort him. When she heard about him, she arose and went to him saying: "My brother, I rejoice with you today because of the pains that you got for the name of our Lord Jesus Christ. The pain of this time is easy comparing with the repose that you will get. It remains forever from the Lord our God." She said this while she was sitting with him to comfort and to strengthen him till the second part of the night, he blessed her, and she went out from (his cell). When it was the eve of

Monday the 16th of Baunah, while he was standing for prayer, our Lord Christ, appeared to him, like a luminous man and holding in his hand an open book and said: "Peace be with you My beloved George, the sweet name in the mouth of everyone. Be strong and be comforted, all your pains and suffering that you received for My name 's sake are written in this book. Raise your eyes and look." The saint rose his eyes and saw a beautiful young man standing and girdled like a great king followed by a great multitude wearing white clothes like snow. [19] All of Them worshipped to the one who had the book. The saint told him: "Who is this great king, that was followed by this multitude." The Lord said to him: "This is my beloved George the Palestinian that you are named after him, and about the multitude that follow him these are all the martyrs. They came beseeching on your behalf so that you accomplish your martyrdom." When the Lord said these words, he disappeared from his sight.

The next day, the military commander sent to him saying: "Why are you in this prison? Send to you wife to bring somebody to sponsor you from me and give me twenty Dirhams, so I will leave you and not to deliver to the inhabitants of Demeira to burn you." The saint sent to him saying: "I do not have money and I do not have sponsor so if they want to burn me, or to sink me in the sea." 'Adî spent the whole day repeating the same speech and he did not accept. When it was midnight, of Tuesday, the saint was standing praying and asking the Lord to strengthen him. A luminous man appeared to him holding a bell with holes. The saint said: "What is this bell that you have in your hand, My Lord?" The Luminous man said: "This is the number of stones that the children and women will stone you." When it was the sixth hour of the day, a news was announced that a message came from Cairo (Misr) to release the saint and

---

19 Inspired by the Apocalypse 13:8, 14:7, 19:10

set him free. A group of Muslim assembled and shouting saying: "If this happens, we all die and not to release him, but let us take him out. Let us ignite a fireplace in the windmill and burn him alive." There was a man present at that time, he was the one who brought the message to Demeira, so he said to them: "Do not do this matter, lest you will be ashamed, as I saw in Cairo (Misr) two of our denomination became Christian and they led them to the Sultan who wanted to release them, but the Careen did not wish to do. They took them out to the marked and burned them and killed them and they spent two days burning them, but the fire did not consume anything from their bodies. When they were ashamed, they gave them to the Christians, so they took them and buried them."

When the multitude heard this, they ceased to this speech. When it was Wednesday, 'Adî rode his riding animal and came to the seashore. A great multitude of Muslims followed him. They assembled with him and adjured him by the life Baraz to deliver this man if not 'we will fight either we all die or we kill him' The military commander went out so that not to be present in the place of war (sedition) and swore to them 'I will deliver to you tomorrow'. They were very happy and diffuse the news everywhere in the city. They all assembled at midnight and spent the whole night to the cockcrowing; it was Wednesday to the ninth hour. The saint was in the prison, it was the time of breakfast, some of the beloved brethren entered to him and ate with him some bread. While eating, a great multitude of Muslims assembled and troubled the whole district. The brethren monk, who were with the saint, became afraid and fled. The jailors closed the prison. The Muslims went to the Military commander, they were shouting. When the saint heard their voices, he stood and spread his hands and prayed saying: "My Lord, strengthen me to put to shame these enemies resisting to your Holy Cross." While the saint was praying, the Muslims were with the Military commander asking to get to the saint to kill him quickly. The governor said to them: "The day is over, and you cannot get what you want but go to him and frighten him so perhaps you can please his heart and he converts. If he refused, come early to me and I deliver to you to do your wish." They hastened to the prison wherein the saint was, and they looked, they saw the saint standing between angels praying. When they saw him, they thought that one of the Christians visiting him. So, some of them stood next to the door guarding him while the rest went to the governor to inform him. They said to him: "Our lord, we went to the prison, and we found some Christians with him praying." When he heard this discourse, he became very angry and said to them: "Go to the prison whoever you will find with him bring their heads and leave their bodies in the prison." When they heard this, they became very happy to hasten to the prison. When they opened and entered, they did not find anybody except the saint alone. They became very amazed and said: "By the life of the Sultan, if you do not return to our religion, we will burn you alive." The saint laughed at their faces and said to them: "You will not make me afraid, O lost, I am rea to die for the name of Jesus Christ, the Son of the Living God forever's sake."

Final Combat

When they heard these words, they said: "We will not leave him forever so that he may escape from us." The saint said to them: "I cannot escape from the service of the Lord. I am ready to do it." They did not believe him, and they delivered him to a monk named Mina, so he sponsored him, and he did not let them to torture him. As for the faithful Christians, when they heard that the saint will accomplish his martyrdom the next day, they brought to him precious wine and pure bread and a flask full of perfume and rose oil and carefully anointed him so that the smell poured. They asked him to eat with them the bread and to bless them. The saint comforted them and ate with them with the joy. When they finished eating, they went in peace to their houses. When it was the third part of the night, he sent (through) the nunnery to his wife, calling her and talked to her saying: "I ask you, my sister neither to come nor to go out with me on this day, because on this day they want to kill me. Do not go out, so these evil men will see you and kill you. But in an elevated place and watch what is happening to me." She replied, while crying: "My brother, and my lord, I ask you do not forget me in your meeting with the Lord Christ." The saint put his hand on her face and signed it with the sign of Cross saying: "Lord Jesus Christ will reward your pains that you endured with me in this time. I will beseech for you, and I farewell you in peace. Me, too, remember me so that the Lord helps me to accomplish my martyrdom." When he said this word, she became troubled and bowed to his legs and kissed feet and said in front of him:

"Be comforted, by brother and be strong and look to the Lord and to yourself so not to fear from death let not spoil what happened this time. You know my brother that the death is for l all us. Finally, you should endure the fear of these evil men better than the terrors of the angels, the changed faces they torture the spirits of the sinners in the sea of the fiery fire for that who deny Christ in the World because of the fear of men. As the worms will not die and their fire did not extinguish forever." While she was talking to him with this speech, it was the sunrise, and it was morning. He said to her: "Go, my sister from here as it is the time that the evil will come. "May Christ bless you that you comforted my spirit in this brief time that I spent with you. You console my soul from the torture." She kissed him and went out from him weeping. A messenger from the devil, announcer of the evil things, the destroyer of spirit, I mean the jailor entered to him shouting saying: "If you obey me and return to the religion of your fathers, I will talk to the multitude on your behalf that you repent from your astray so, I may deliver you from them, as I see them coming and their anger is like fire." The saint replied to him: "16:23 Get you behind me, cursed Satan[20] : I do not care about you and your discourse for the death of this world I chose for myself."

While the evil talking with him, the multitude came so that the city was shaken like an earthquake from their sounds. When the saint heard them, knew that his time was approaching. So, on the spot, he took water and washed himself with the rest of perfume and the rose oil that the Christians brought it. He anointed himself and bowed himself three times saying: "My God and my Lord Jesus Christ, this is the time that I was waiting for to accomplish my martyrdom. I ask you my Lord to send me your divine Strength and Holy Spirit and do not put Your slave to shame today among these evil multitude. To You is the Glory, the power forever Amen." When he said this, he signed himself with the sing of the Cross, he took the cloth that was on his head and divided into two parts. He took half and girded himself and the other put it around his head. A man from Masmud whose name Abu al-Hassan came followed by the second Galaad, I mean Mansur, the lefthanded slave who is dwelling in Al-Daruwathin, entered to the saint saying: "My son, you know that I am a friend of your father. He entrusted me to care about you and your brethren, now I know that you did not do this by your own will but your wife that indicated this to you. Now my son, listen to mem as I am the companion of your father, and he entrusted me to care about you and your brethren. Now listen to me, return to our religion and I will deliver you from them.

---

20 Mat 16:23.

I will make you a military commander and the leaders will greatly honour." The saint told him: "You will be burned your and all your sons in the fire furnace forever. You are not my father, and I am not your son. I am foreign from you, and you are foreign from me in this age and the coming age. I am openly Christian. I am the slave of Jesus Christ." The slave of Mansur lifted his hand with guile and stroke the blessed face of the saint. Then he loosened his feet from the wooden beam and took him out to the multitude. He (the saint) was glorifying God, the light of God was covering him. When the evil (men) saw him, they gnashed of their teeth, like fierce lions and they replied saying: "What should we do with this (man)" Some of them said: "let us burn him with fire." While others said: "Let us stone him with rocks." The saint did not paid attention to this speech as he was thinking to the heavenly matters. They took him out and they were surrounding him, and they brought him to the Mosque, where they used to pray. The saint was above all as testified his wife Saywālā and said: "I was on the roof, and I saw him above all who were surrounding him." When they reached the Mosque, 'Adî and Baraz the deputy and the judge of the district and all the sheiks said to him: "Muzahim, can you see the anger of this multitude because of you, but for our love to you, We will not deliver you to them. We took you here to our Mosque and by the life of the Sultan, if you listen to us, every one of us will give you a horse and a garment and three servants and three dinars, and whatever you want from us/ We will be your friend and you will eat and drink with us and we will make you a councillor. Do not destroy your youth." The saint cried as much as he can: "My Lord Jesus Christ, the Son of the Living God help me!" When they heard this, they took his cloth and whipped him so that his blood shed on earth. They mercilessly hit him, and they took him the place of his martyrdom, the place that our Lord Jesus Christ shew him in the vision. They surrounded his to kill him, they lifted their eyes and saw a camel man. He ordered to bring him to them. The military commander and the leaders ordered not to quickly kill him but to be patient in their tortures so he may return. He ordered to loosen the leading rope of the four camels, and they folded them seven times and they stood in front and behind him and they gave him a sound beating without mercy. Some other wished to beat him with staff as it would be better for them. As the Lord said in His Holy Gospel: "the time comes, that whosoever kill you will think that he does God service."[21] That what the evil did with the saint. They surrounded him, holding staffs in their hands, spears, and swords. It was said that one thousand five hundred were around the saint. As for who had beaten him with staff, they did not cease to do it. The saint did not utter anything except the name of the Lord Jesus Christ. When the leader saw his endurance, he wanted to leave him, one of the leaders of the city, whose name was Hadid advanced and said: "By the life of Sultan, if you did not kill him, we will destroy the city." He cried out to the multitude: "Kill him and do not venerate him." They jumped on his with the spears and swords and the big nails and the iron rods and all weapons that can bring they used it to beat him. After all these, the saint did not die. He did not turn his face right or left. He did not cease to meditate the name of the Lord Jesus Christ. The multitude was amazed saying: "All what we did not die." By the end, some of them said: "His God, that he meditates by mouth, did not let him die.

One of them took a stone and stuffed in the saint's mouth, and blocked his mouth, not to let him to mention this Name. As for the saint, he did not cease to mention the name of the Lord Christ in his heart. Then, an evil servant, riding a horse, who were among the people with 'Adî, advanced with a spear in his

---

21 Jn 16:2

hand, he expelled all who were surrounding him (the saint), and pierced the saint in his heart, till it appeared from his back. The saint became diminished in his spirit, so he turned his face towards the East, signed his face with the Cross. When the evil saw that he did not die, Hadid, the evil said: "If we tortured him many times like this and we will not severe his head, he would not die." The evil went away from him and started to discuss how to kill him.

The saint stood and lifted his hands to heaven and said: "I thank you my Lord, my Saviour Jesus Christ for you make me worthy to suffer for Your Holy name's sake, like the other martyrs. I beseech you my Lord, to send me the archangel Michael to stay with me till I deliver my soul to Your Hands. To You is the glory, the power, the might forever and ever Amen!" When he finished his prayer: Lord and Saviour Jesus Christ appeared to him saying: "Come to me, my beloved George, inherit the kingdom prepared for you from the foundation of the world[22] Be strong I Am with you till you accomplish your martyrdom. I prepared for your three crowns in the hand of Michael the Archangel, one for your love to me and your baptism, the second one for the tortures that you received for My Name's sake, the third for your accomplishment of your true martyrdom. You revealed My Name in front of all the world, I will reveal you in front My Father who is in Heavens and His angels. Whoever will take your body and shroud, I will cloth him with the heavenly garments. Whoever will build a church after your name I will adorn for him a house in my kingdom, and I will let dwell in the eternal joy. Whoever will give alms for your name, I will satisfy from the heavenly good. Whoever will sponsor the writing of your martyrdom and reveal the tortures that you get for My name's sake, I will write his name in the book of life with all the

---

22 Mat 25:34

saints. And whosoever shall give to drink a cup of cold [water][23] for your name, he will not lose his reward. Lift your eyes to the sky and you will see all ranks of the Angels the Martyrs and the saints came to see the accomplishment of your martyrdom. Do not fear, my beloved George. The hour of your martyrdom is approaching." Upon saying this, the Saviour gave him peace and ascended to heavens while he (the saint) was watching. When the saint saw this, he rejoiced in the Spirit and said: "Who am I so that You appeared to me, my Lord, my Saviour, to appear by this speech." While he was thinking about this, he saw an evil man and advancing, he gave him a sound beating with the sword, three times. The sword did not cut anything, the people were amazed for this time. Another evil man bet him with the sword on his head gouged his head and his brain and he stretched his hand and took the brain, played with it with his hand and threw the sea. He took a stone and continued to hit his head until he crushed out. On the spot, he (the saint) delivered his spirit in the hands of the Lord in the third hour of Thursday the 19th of Baunah in the year 695 of the martyrs during the reign of Baraz, in his third year of his reign. May the intercession of this saint be with us and preserve us from the snares of the enemy and all the children of Baptistery.

And also we explain to you my brethren the miracle of the saint George Muzahim, my his intercession be with us amen!

Martyrdom And The Relics

When they saw that he died, they rejoiced with happiness, and they brought baskets and shovels and dug the traces of his blood, and they collected him and threw him in the sea. They put make his feet in a rope to a pond next to the seashore. They

---

23 Mat 10:42

collected thorns and wood, and they made a huge hill on the body of the saint. They made fire to burn him. On the spot, his body jumped over the fire, and everybody were amazed and were greatly trembled. Then, the saint turned his face to the East and sat in the midst of the fire. They became very afraid that someone may see him. Some of them went to a boat and took him with the rope and bound the neck of the saint and put him on the fire. So, water came out of the body of saint and extinguished the water. When the evil saw this miracle that his body was not burned at all, he became very any and replying saying: "Woe to us all if the body is not burned, we will be all in great shame. He renewed and swore that he will not leave this place even if he will stay for three days till the body will be burned and to throw his ashes in the sea. Therefore, he sat being possessed by anger next to the seashore. There was a great palm tree thrown there, so he sent and bought from its owner for three dinars. He ordered a group of men to carry it to the boat. They crossed with it to where the body of the saint. They brought the carpenters with the hammers and cut the palm tree and they put it around the body of the saint. The palm tree was entirely consumed but the body did not burn. While the evil was thinking and worried about the miracles that happened from the body of the Saint, 'Adî, the military commander and Bašîr the Armenian the keeper of his gate came from Al-Dawritin with their servant in front of them.

When they reached the seashore where the body of the saint was there, and they were burning it. They asked the men who were present about the body of the saint. They informed them that they greatly pained, and they were unable to burn. So, 'Adî and Bašîr told them: "We did not cease to tell you that and you did not listen to us, now you are ashamed." When they heard this speech, they became very angry. They sent to buy Sulphur and asphalt and raw iron to his mill. He brought bread of radish and ordered to cut the belly of the saint and to take everything inside and to throw in the fire. They took out the liver and the fat and they put it in the fire. On the spot, it extinguished the fire. He ordered to bring butcher and to cut his members and to separate from each. They cut his arms from his elbows, and his feet from his knees and they put them inside his belly. He ordered to take two pieces of woods and to paint them with asphalt and to put them in his ribs right and left, they make him to sit on a seat and put around him wood and filled his belly with asphalt and sulphur. They ignited fire and there was a great fire. They did burn as the Merciful Lord overshadowed over his body so that the fire did not burn his body. When they saw that his body did not burn, they became very worried and he ordered the butchers to cut his body into pieces. God knows the number of pieces that they cut from his body and they spread the wood and the weeds and they put the pieces of the body of the saint on them layer by layer. They put over them the wood and the asphalt and the sulphur.

They ignited fire and nothing from them were burned but put them on shame from the third hour to the ninth hour. The evil (men) took a council saying: "If we leave these members thrown, the Christians will come and see them and put us in shame. So, let us a basket and put the body in it and go to the furnace of the bath so if they are not burned, we will throw them in the sea." When they said this, they carried the basked which contained the members of the saint, and they came up to the boat. On the spot, a great agitation took place in the boat that they were about to sink. So, they took the basked and throw it in the sea. The basket floated on the sea surface. When the evil who were in the boat saw that, they became very troubled, and they ordered some of them to go in the sea and to cut the basket into two pieces and to sink it in the water. They did that, so, the evil (men) were very happy, they danced and the herald cried out saying: "O people, whoever wants to become Christian look to this." The evil of the inhabitants of Demeira that he sunk and they used to walk in the place where the saint was killed to the East, laughing saying: "We finished to kill him." When the saint, his wife, saw the accomplishment of his martyrdom and the throwing of his body in the sea, she went to the cell of the nuns crying and saying: "Woe to me my brother George for from the time that I was with you from a place to another and these evil people torturing you. I used to comfort you and made you as ease till you accomplished your martyrdom and I take you body to be my refuge and to strengthen me till the day of my death. Woe to me, and woe to me as my hope was loosed and I do not find any small piece of your holy body." While she was seeping, a Christian woman knocked at the door of the door of the nuns saying: "O Saywālā, may God increase your comfort, take this part from the body of your husband as my son brought it to give it to you to become a consolation and comfort to the day of your death. But be sure in all your heart that the grace of God and his saint in this part." When she took it with great joy and happiness as if she found a great gain as she loved. Then she took it wrapped in a white cloth, kissed, and went to her house and put perfume on it. She made a coffin and she lite a candle shining day and night. The fame of the saint became everywhere. Everyone used to come to bring sacrifice and get blessing from it and kissing his body. The information reached his mother in the city called Tantah that he accomplished his martyrdom in Demeira, she tore her clothes and wept saying: "Woe to me my beloved son, the light of my eyes, the joy of my soul became grief. I wished that I was next to you and see your death. Woe to me, a weak woman and if I know your way or your place. I would ask a man to walk with me to get the news of my son, but I did it find." Then, she went out to the street by herself and she found two ways, she did not know which one.

She sat down weeping and thinking about her matter. While she was weeping in such manner, the angel of the Lord Gabriel, in the shape of a man walking. He stopped next to her and said to her: "My mother Mary, why are you sitting weeping?" She said: "I am looking for a man to walk with me to Demeira to visit my son, as I heard that was killed." Then she said: "Who are you and how do you know my name?" He said: "I am Gabriel the angel, the friend of your son since his childhood. I will walk with you to wherever you want." Then, he walked with her and she was following him till he made her to cross to Sundufa and there she found faithful people going to Demeira so he left her with them and recommended her to them. He was then lifted to heaven, while she was looking at him. She testified and swore, by the great faiths that during all her walking with him in the street, she did not feel any pain or fear. That is what she testified it for us, the mother of the saint and his wife. A man, monk, called Mina, whose the Lord sent him to the saint to strengthen him and to make him an ease like Samuel with saint Apater, who testified the accomplishment of the martyrdom of the saint and all what took place to this saint, George the second. We know that his testimony is true.[24]

Epilogue

We all who are present on this feast today, beseech the Lord to accept the intercession of the saint for the forgiveness of our sins in front of the tribune of our Lord, our Saviour Jesus Christ, on the day of Judgement where He will give everyone according to his deeds. To Whom is the glory and honour and sanctification and might and greatness and omnipotence to His Merciful and Clement Father and the Life-give Holy Spirit.

---

24 Jn 21L: 24

The Consubstantial with the Father, and the Son Forever and ever Amen!

May the Lord make us, and you reach this feast for many years and continued years and to deliver us from the snares of the devil and his traps and make us to hear the joyful voice saying: "Come, you blessed of my Father, inherit the kingdom prepared for you from the foundation of the world." [25]

Through the intercession of the Holy Lady, the pure, virtuous Mistress Mary and the intercession of the angels standing in front of the Mighty Divinity for the spiritual praise and the intercession of all the saints, the pure saints and the just martyrs. Amen!

Finished the martyrdom of honoured saint George the second, known as Muzahim , may the Lord grant us all his intercession. Amen!

---

25 Mat 25: 34

Scan the QR code to go to our
website where you will find

- Book reviews

- Great deals

- Our full library

  of books

SCAN ME